POEMS FROM A WIDOW'S HEART

SALLY JADLOW

Scripture quotations taken from the New American Standard Bible® (NASB), Copyright © 1960, 1962, 1963, 1968, 1971, 1972, 1973, 1975, 1977, 1995 by The Lockman Foundation Used by permission. www.Lockman.org

Independently Published.

Cover design by MJ Freeman of Valiant Courier Publications
Printed in the United States of America

DEDICATION

This book is dedicated to my Unseen Husband who knows me best
and loves me most and to my seen husband who loved me well

.

Table of Contents

Foreword

I became a widow April 21, 2018. As my husband Vic and I walked his last mile together, I journaled each step of the way. Sometimes my words came out of my heart and onto the page in poetry, sometimes in prose.

This collection of poetry is a harvest of that time. It is my hope that you find some comfort or fresh insight in these pages.

I took the photo for the cover for this book of a sunset while off the coast of Maine on our last cruise together just seven months before he died. At that time, we had no idea lung cancer was alive and well throughout his body.

Sally Jadlow
June 3, 2020

Portrait of an Illness

He suffers a sore hip.
Is it arthritis?
Seek wisdom of doctors
for several months.
Finally, MRIs reveal cancer.
Biopsy pinpoints origin in lung.
PET scan shows growth
metastasized to bones
and beyond.
Diagnosis: stage 4.
Inoperable.

Psalm 103:1-3 Bless the Lord, O my soul;
And all that is within me, bless His holy name.
Bless the Lord, O my soul,
And forget none of His benefits;
Who pardons all your iniquities;
Who heals all your diseases;
Who redeems your life from the pit;

The Racer

The finish line's in sight—
little doubt what he'll die of.

As to when,
that's still unknown.

How we get there is the mystery.
Who we choose to lean on is certain.

Psalm 25:15   My eyes are continually toward the Lord,
For He will pluck my feet out of the net.

In the Midst of the Storm

Even in the darkest night
I will raise my voice in praise.
My hands will still be raised,
to the One who ever watches
the sheep of His pasture—
His own, ever after.

Psalm 34:1b & 4   I will bless the Lord at all times;
His praise shall continually be in my mouth.
I sought the Lord, and He answered me,
And delivered me from all my fears.

The Diagnosis

The doctor says,
"We've done all we can do."
The patient turns in grief,
then realizes,
what the world sees as worst
is really the best.
Graduation day is in view.

Revelation 21:2 And I saw the holy city, new Jerusalem, coming down out of heaven from God, made ready as a bride adorned for her husband.

Long-Term Caretaking

Dreaded illness holds loved-one
in its clutches
as we watch, pray, and hope.

As weeks turn into months
our assignment seems to have no end—
no timetable for the finish line.

Our strength wains,
patience grows thin
as we watch disease take its toll.

We long for the day
our dear one can fly free
of earths' cursed restrictions
and so loose us from
our tiring task.

Psalm 55:22a Cast your burden upon the Lord and He will sustain
you;

Temptation

looms large to take him home
and avoid the hospice hospital
as I follow the transport ambulance.

I grip the wheel
as we pass our exit to home,
fight to yield to the temptation to scream
at the ambulance driver,
"Turn off here! Go this way!"

A tear escapes my eye
for he'll not pass this way again.

Psalm 147:3   He heals the brokenhearted
             And binds up their wounds.

Darkest Hour

When your hang-on is all gone,
and you feel you can't take another step,
pause, take a deep breath, and pray.

Rest in the thought, Mary, Jake or John,
you are loved with deep depth,
more than any words can say

By the One who you may call on
who supplies your every breath
each hour of every day.

Psalm 119:114 & 116
        You are my hiding place and my shield;
        I wait for Your word.
        Sustain me according to Your word, that I may live'
        And do not let me be ashamed of my hope.

Love Poem

My dear husband of fifty-six years,
I watch you as you sleep
remembering the good times and bad.

Barring a miraculous recovery,
you'll leave earth soon.
I'll go forth on my own—
and yet, I'll not be alone.

Jesus has promised to be my husband
in your absence.

Until we meet again, dear one,
be blessed in His presence.

Isaiah 54:5-6
> "For your husband is your Maker,
> Whose name is the Lord of hosts;
> And your Redeemer is the Holy One of Israel,
> Who is called the God of all the earth.
> For the Lord has called you,
> Like a wife forsaken and grieved in spirit,
> Even like a wife of one's youth when she is rejected,"
> Says your God.

Proposition

Cancer, how about
You go away, and we'll forget
All the indignities,
All the pain,
All the grief.

Cancer answers,
"No deal!"

Job 13:15   Though He slay me,
                 I will hope in Him.

Time

flies by
when no one is looking.

In the beginning
we think we have a mountain of days.
All the while each one slips by
out of sight,
out of mind,
until we have a precious few
left in a tiny pile.

Our remaining words escape unsaid,
thoughts unshared,
dreams unlived
until we come to the last one together here.

Ecclesiastes 11:10 So, remove grief and anger from your heart and
put away pain from your body, because childhood and the prime of
life are fleeting.

Sweet Chariot

"Go get the wagon!" he says.
"The wagon?"
"Yes. Go get it!"

He holds out his hand and says,
"Here. Take the reins."
In confusion, I pretend to take them.
"Don't just stand there.
Take them outside."
I slap the air as if hitting a haunch
and say, "Yah! Get outta here!"

He lays his head back on the pillow
and closes his eyes.
I wonder if my sweet farmer will cross
the Jordan in a buckboard.

Psalm 31:24   Be strong, and let your heart take courage,
                       All you who hope in the Lord.

Take the Reins

He says as he holds out his hand
in the Hospice Hospital.

Is he leaving now?
How can I take the reins?
My hands aren't big enough.
Please stay longer.

Guilt overwhelms me.
It's my selfish desire
to keep him here with me
in pain,
rather than let him go Home
to healing and sweet relief.

Philippians 4:13 I can do all things through Him who strengthens
me.

A Thin Thread

tethers loved one to this earth.
He stares at his new surroundings
at Hospice House.

I pray the angels come soon
to cut the thin thread
and release him to ride home
in their sweet chariot.

II Corinthians 5:6,8   Therefore being always of good courage, and knowing that while we are at home in the body we are absent from the Lord—we are of good courage, I say, and prefer rather to be absent from the body and to be at home with the Lord.

Jealous of You

who got to go to heaven without me.
Wishing we could have gone together.
Hoping for a quick escape from earth
for those left behind.

I Thessalonians 4:17 Then we who are alive and remain will be
caught up together with them in the clouds to meet the Lord in the
air, and so we shall always be with the Lord.

When I See You Again, My Dear

the effects of the fall will be no more.
Things will be as God intended
before the serpent had his say.

When I see you again, my dear,
we'll have bodies which will never grow old
and night will be eternal day.

When I see you again, my dear,
the cares of this world will be no more;
all sighing will have passed away.

When I see you again, my dear,
    good-byes will be a distant memory,
    an archived word, an ancient cliché.

    When I see you again, my dear,
    we'll worship together at the feet of the One
    who had the final say.

Isaiah 35:10   And the ransomed of the Lord will return
    And come with joyful shouting to Zion,
    With everlasting joy upon their heads.
    They will find gladness and joy,
    And sorrow and sighing will flee away.

Shortsighted Seers

weep and wail.
Lament the loss of loved ones
when all the while
a gathering waits giddy
on the other side
to see them again.

1 Peter 1:8-9 and though you have not seen Him, you love him, and though you do not see Him now, but believe in Him, you greatly rejoice with joy inexpressible and full of glory, obtaining as the outcome of your faith the salvation of your souls.

Hidden Date

Each of us is stamped with an expiration date,
known only to Him.

We can't make ourselves live longer
no matter how hard we try.

When our time comes, He'll send the angels
to conduct us home.

The date is not to be feared or dreaded,
only anticipated.

Fill your days to the fullest
so when we stand before Him,

We will hear Him say,
    "Well done!"

Job 14:5 Since his days are determined,
        The number of his months is with You;
        And his limits You have set so that he cannot pass.

God Said It

I believe it.
That's that.

He doesn't tell tall tales
to entertain.

He doesn't make up fairy tales
to fill our heads with fantasies.

He tells us of the unseen
so we might trust the Truth.

Numbers 23:19 God is not man that He should lie—neither is He son of man that He should repent. Has He said and will He not do it? Has He spoken and will He not make it good?

Lead Me, Lord

So many paths before me
in these twilight years.
I glance at each one,
more tempting than the last.
Which will yield the most fruit
in the grand scheme of things?
Which will be the greatest benefit?
I must not tarry here long
lest I miss the moment
in my dithering.

Isaiah 30: 21 Your ears will hear a word behind you, "This is the way, walk in it," whenever you turn to the right or to the left.

Your Unique Space

Each of us has a space to occupy,
a reason to be.
A song to sing,
a vision to see.

We can share what we've been given
or hold it tight to our chest.
I think
sharing is best.

Jeremiah 1:5a Before I formed you in the womb I knew you.
                    And before you were born I consecrated you;

I'm Sorry

I couldn't love you enough
to keep you from dying;
sorry that your book of days ran out
before mine.

I'm sorry our life on earth ended
before our fifty-sixth wedding anniversary.
Sorry you didn't get to stick around to see
our soon-to-come first great-grand child.

I'm sorry for a lot of things,
but not for our lifetime
of joys and sorrows together.

Philippians 4:4 Rejoice in the Lord always; again I will say,
rejoice!

Courage

Soldiers in battle,
persecuted persons,
cancer patients,
all brave.

For some,
facing one more day
is the bravest of all.

Isaiah 41:10
> Do not fear, for I am with you.
> Do not anxiously look about you, for I am your God.
> I will strengthen you, surely I will help you,
> Surely I will uphold you with My righteous right hand.

A Broken Poem

There is no one so broken,
so deep in a pit,
that Jesus cannot heal or rescue.

If He cares for even the sparrows
does He not care even more
for you?

Matthew 6:26 "Look at the birds of the air, that they do not sow, nor reap nor gather into barns, and yet your heavenly Father feeds them. Are you not worth much more than they?

How to Survive the Death of a Spouse

Take a deep breath.
Allow some time to grieve
the absence of your right arm.

Then take another deep breath
while you seek the shape
of your remaining days
until you rejoin your missing appendage.

Psalm 139:16 Your eyes have seen my unformed substance;
And in your book were all written
The days that were ordained for me,
When as yet there was not one of them.

New Nightwear

I spied it on the sale rack in January—
an unpurchased nightgown from Christmas.
Soft brushed cotton
covered with lollipops and candy canes,
a perfect fit except
sleeves and length, too short
for cold winter nights.

I stopped by a fabric store,
took a turn through remnants,
grabbed a bright colored packet,
sewed longer arms and length
to cover ankles and wrists.

Now I'm warm,
snug against winter winds,
alone in my too-wide bed.

Matthew 6:28-30 And why are you worried about clothing? Observe
how the lilies of the field grow; they do not toil nor do they spin, yet
I say to you that not even Solomon in all his glory clothed himself
like one of these. But if God so clothes the grass of the field, which
is alive today and tomorrow is thrown into the furnace, will He not
much more clothe you? You of little faith!

Grief

Lurks in the shadows,
waiting, watching
for an unexpected time
when it pops out,
bites your behind,
and takes a chunk
before it disappears
into thin air
leaving you heaving for breath,
your backside bruised,
and your confidence crushed.

Psalm 3:2-3   Many are saying of my soul,
"There is not deliverance for him in God."
But You, O Lord, are a shield about me,
My glory, and the One who lifts my head.

Sixteen Weeks

It's Saturday again—
the day Vic went to heaven.

He shed his cancer-ridden earth suit
and flew the coop,

leaving behind life and all its troubles
and entered eternity's bubble.

How I wish I could have grabbed his coat-tail
and accompanied him down that trail.

Revelation 22:17 The Spirit and the bride say, "Come." And let the one who hears say, "Come." And let the one who is thirsty come; let the one who wishes take the water of life without cost.

My Love

Seven months ago
I could still say,
"I love you"
and you could hear the words.

Now, I'm not so sure
if those in heaven can hear
things uttered on Earth
but I'll utter it anyway,

just in case you can.

Hebrews 12:1 Therefore, since we have so great a cloud of
witnesses surrounding us, let us also lay aside every encumbrance
and the sin which so easily entangles us, and let us run with
endurance the race that is set before us,

After a Year

Living alone takes a cup full of determination,
a bucket of planning,
and an ocean of God's grace.

Do you wonder how I know?
Because I've been measuring cupsful,
Toting buckets,
and swimming for 357 days.

Galatians 6:9 Let us not lose heart in doing good, for in due time we
will reap if we do not grow weary.

Easter Morn

Darkness turned to dawn
the day Jesus rose from the grave.

Despair turned to disbelief
when Mary Magdalene brought the news,
"He is risen!"

Frantic confusion gave way to faith
when Peter and John entered
the empty tomb.

Aching hearts healed
when two followers broke bread
in Emmaus with their risen Lord Jesus.

Has darkness turned to dawn
in your heart, dear friend?

Luke 24:38-39 And He said to them, "Why are you troubled, and
why do doubts arise in your hearts? See My hands and My feet, that
it is I Myself; touch Me and see, for a spirit does not have flesh and
bones as you see that I have."

How Long, Lord Jesus?

How many years do I have to wait
before I can see Your beautiful face?

How many days must pass by
before I can see You eye to eye?

How many minutes have to tick away
Before I can hear You say,

"Well done, my friend, well done!"

Revelation 12:10 Then I heard a loud voice in heaven, saying, "Now the salvation, and the power, and the kingdom of our God and the authority of His Christ have come, for the accuser of our brethren has been thrown down, he who accuses them before our God day and night.

Made to Thrive

Through good times and bad
I have drawn the Living Water
from the earth,
ever pushing deeper to anchor
in His good soil
that I may produce much fruit
to glorify the One who planted me.

Psalm 1:3
> He will be like a tree firmly planted by streams of water,
> Which yields its fruit in its season
> And its leaf does not wither;
> And in whatever he does, he prospers.

The Widow's Song

Don't weep for me, dear friends,
for I was loved long and well.
He cherished me deeply
before he fell.

This one thing I ask of you.
Listen with all your heart.
Love yours still among the living.
You never know when they'll depart.

Psalm 90:12   So teach us to number our days,
That we may present to You a heart of wisdom.

Widow's Love Poem

I miss the feel of your strong arm around my shoulder,
the deep timbre of your voice,
and your expert wisdom in all things.

One day, I will again behold you face to face
on a distant shore
in a land of no good-byes.

Until that day,
I will remember you with a longing heart,
sweet memories, and an undying love.

Song of Solomon 2:14   O my dove, in the clefts of the rock
In the secret place of the steep pathway,
Let me see your form,
Let me hear your voice;
For you voice is sweet,
And your form is lovely.

One Day

Today, one day closer to eternity.

Some folks dread
one day closer to eternity.

Others long for that day,
one day closer to eternity.

For me, I mark the calendar
one day closer to eternity

to see my beloved rejoicing in eternity.

Revelation 22:5 And there will no longer be any night; and they will
not have need of the light of a lamp nor the light of the sun, because
the Lord God will illumine them; and they will reign forever and
ever.

I Wish

we were all home in heaven
where tears are no more,
pain is banished,
and all are without
the stain of sin.

Where things are as before
Adam and Eve fell.
Where we are face-to-face
with our Creator, Father God,
where time has lost its power
and darkness is no more.

Revelation 21:3-4 And I heard a loud voice from the throne, saying, "Behold, the tabernacle of God is among men, and He will dwell among them, and they shall be His people, and God Himself will be among them and He will wipe away every tear form their eyes; and there will no longer be any death; there will no longer be any mourning, or crying, or pain; the first things have passed away."

The Tale-Keeper

My love, I will keep your stories alive
retelling to those left behind
of your tales of the cockleburs
placed in the teacher's hairnet
in your one-room country grade school.

I'll share how you got your tongue stuck
on the pipe hand-rail on the bridge
near your home in winter,
and caught crawdads there in summer.

I'll recall how you learned
to plow a straight row with a team of horses
when you were only nine.

I'll relay the story about how you and the other boys
tipped over the outhouse on Halloween,
chopped wood for the pot-bellied stove,
played ball in the schoolyard at lunch.
walked to school in all weather,
and learned about places far from your
Kansas farm home.

I'll tell them of your dog Troubles
and your paint horse Dixie and how you
drove the milk to town each morning
on your way to high school.

I'll remind them of the fine man
their grandpa was to the very end.

John 15:17 "This I command you, that you love one another."

About the Author

Sally Jadlow is a corporate chaplain and an award-winning professional writer. She and her husband Vic were married for almost fifty-six years and lived in the suburbs of Kansas City. They were parents to four children, fourteen grandchildren, and one great-grandchild.

She teaches children and adults the finer points of writing. Sally is available to speak on many inspirational and writing subjects.

You can find Sally's website at www.SallyJadlow.com.

Other works by Sally Jadlow available in paperback and e-reader.
Amazon Author Page: https://www.amazon.com/-/e/B007F5H0H4

The Road Home
Sally Jadlow's first-hand, no-holds-barred account of her husband's illness and God's faithfulness.

The Late Sooner
The first of her Heartland trilogy. Sanford Deering, staked a claim in the Oklahoma Territory in the first land run of 1889. The novel is based on Sanford's actual one-line-a-day diary in early Oklahoma. Sanford is Sally's great-grandfather.

The Late Sooner's Daughter
The second book in the series. Nora Deering, Sanford's daughter, accompanies her family back to Missouri. How will she find true love in this new place and overcome her hidden fear?

Hard Times in the Heartland
The conclusion of her Heartland trilogy. Henry, eldest of Nora's six sons, is faced with headship of the clan at twenty-three when his mother dies in 1933. How will he care for his youngest brother, David, age eleven, and keep their family together? Based on Henry's letters from WW II in Germany.

God's Little Miracle Book I, II, III
Each book contains twenty-seven true stories of God's intervention in the lives of every-day people.

Joshua's Journey: One Boy's Victory Over Allergies

Joshua's parents couldn't understand why their son couldn't learn, print legibly, or control bizarre behavior. After ten long years of frustration, a chance TV program provided long sought-after answers.

Daily Walk with Jesus

Co-authored with Ardythe Kolb, this book contains 365 daily devotionals complete with a scripture of the day and a prayer for a great way to start your day.

Looking Deeper-A 366 Day Devotional

Inspiring scripture devotional digging deep into the words' original meanings. There is room for the reader to jot notes.

Family Favorites from the Heartland

Over 100 delicious recipes to please the palate, tested on family members and friends for over fifty-five years. Simple, easy-to-follow instructions. A great gift for a new bride or an experienced cook looking for fresh ideas.

Sonflower Seeds

Sonflower Seeds is a varied collection of poems and inspirational short stories. Awarded Best Book of Poetry at Oklahoma Writers Federation, Inc. in 2002.

Please Leave Me a Review!

If you enjoyed this book or found it useful, please take a moment to leave a review on Amazon. I'm always interested in learning what you like, think and want. I read all the reviews personally.

https://www.amazon.com/-/e/B007F5H0H4
Thank you for your support!